D0605941

THE GUARDIAN TEAM

RENA AND ROO

THE GUARDIAN TEAM

ON THE JOB WITH RENA AND ROO

CAT URBIGKIT

BOYDS MILLS PRESS
AN IMPRINT OF HIGHLIGHTS
Honesdale, Pennsylvania

She was the littlest, scraggliest wild burro in the bunch. Almost one year old, she had become an orphan after she was separated from her wild-burro mother on the dry desert rangeland of Nevada. The burro was moved to a quiet ranch in Wyoming to begin a new life. She was named Roo.

The pup was the runt of a litter of seven. Though she was the smallest, she was constantly in fights with her bigger brothers and sisters. The pup was brought to the ranch when she was three months old. She was named Rena.

Rena and Roo would soon begin important jobs. They would become livestock guardians, in charge of protecting lambs from predators such as coyotes.

The lambs were orphans. Somehow, they had become separated from their mothers out on the range. The newborn lambs were moved to a pen on the ranch. The animals would grow up there and be well cared for.

When Rena met the lambs, she licked their faces.

Livestock guardians like Rena develop close relationships with the animals they guard, and this usually begins when the animals are very young. The development of this connection between animals is called bonding.

When Roo arrived at the ranch, she was led over to the lambs for an introduction.

They were all scared, but they were also curious about each other.

Soon Roo and the lambs were running around in the pen. After a few laps, they got tired and took a break.

Then it was time for the hard part—introducing Roo to Rena. Both were scared, so they watched each other for awhile during their first short visit.

The process of introducing new animals to each other is called socialization. During this process, animals learn that what might seem scary really isn't scary after all.

By the next morning, Roo seemed to enjoy being with the lambs. She was careful not to step on them when they walked underneath her. The lambs' morning bucket of milk was put in the pen, and Roo figured out how to get her share as the lambs sucked on the nipples of the bucket.

When Rena entered the pen for another visit, Roo walked over to investigate the pup. Rena was scared of the burro, but the dog insisted on visiting her lamb pals. Roo was a natural guardian, trying to keep Rena away from the lambs.

Rena stood up to Roo, even though Roo was much bigger.
The pup did not give up, and she eventually got to spend
time with the lambs.

After a few days, the animals were let out into a big pasture. Rena and Roo continued to disagree about who should guard the lambs.

When a lamb wandered too far from the others,
Roo chased it back to the bunch.

Rena guarded the lambs by staying with them, barking if she sensed danger. As the days went by, the lambs grew bigger and stronger, and the loose wool covering their bodies started growing into thick coats.

Livestock guardian animals, including burros and
guard dogs, live with their sheep herds year-round.
Burros will chase any predator that comes near their herd,
while the sound of a dog's loud bark will also turn most
predators away.

One afternoon, an adult male sheep, called a ram, ambled over to see the lambs. Unsure of what to do, Roo met the ram face-to-face. She decided that the ram shouldn't be trusted, so from then on, she worked to keep him away from her flock.

As they lived together with the lambs, Rena and Roo finally began to share the work of guarding. Sometimes while the lambs would nap, Rena would sit on the steps of the ranch house, with Roo standing nearby, and they would play-fight, gently nipping and teasing each other.

The livestock guardians had become friends.

While the guardians played and patrolled for danger, their bodies grew. Roo got bigger, and her scraggly hair started to fall away, revealing the muscular animal beneath.

Rena's puppy teeth fell out and were replaced with her bigger adult teeth. The pup gradually got taller and longer, growing into a graceful, athletic dog.

Rena helped Roo to keep the ram away from the lambs. If Roo didn't want him around, Rena would help.

24

The lambs benefited from all the good care. They raced, leaped, and munched and were unharmed by predators because there was always a guardian nearby. The orphans were growing into beautiful adults.

As fall changed to winter, the animals settled into a routine. Roo would often lead the herd around the pasture during the day, with Rena following along behind.

The sheep were fed hay every day in the winter, and
Rena and Roo would watch over them as they ate. Once
their tummies were full, the lambs took afternoon naps.

The lambs had finally grown large enough to join the ranch's big herd. Roo went with the sheep to help guard them, but Rena stayed where she was, ready to take on a new job. She would go visit Roo and the big herd every now and then, but she was soon very busy.

The arrival of spring meant another lambing season had arrived. A few newborn lambs had become separated from their mothers and were sent to the small pen on the ranch. Rena would have to watch over these new babies, and Rena knew just what to do. She would become their guardian, and keep them safe.

Author's Note

Burro is the Spanish word for the wild donkeys that live out on the range in the western United States, sharing land with herds of wild horses. To keep the herds small enough so they don't overgraze the range, government officials gather and offer excess wild horses and burros for adoption. Sheep ranchers have discovered that the burro's natural guarding instinct makes the animal ideal for watching over domestic sheep.

Livestock guardian dogs like Rena have been used to guard sheep for thousands of years in central Asia and other parts of the world, and they are now used to watch over livestock herds in the United States.

I live on a ranch in Wyoming along with my family and the animals that appear in this book. It is a pleasure to walk out to the herd and have the dogs run to me for affection, while the burros dig in my pockets for treats and the lambs approach me for some attention.

We know that our herd is very well protected when the sheep are with the burros and dogs, and we consider these animals our working partners as well as dear friends. One thing all three species have in common is that they are social animals. Just as a pet cat or dog likes to receive rubs and attention, so do these burros and working dogs that share our ranch and live with us.

—C.U.

Bibliography

Andelt, William F. "Use of Livestock Guardian Animals to Reduce Predation on Sheep and Livestock." *Sheep and Goat Research Journal* 19 (2004): 72–75.

Dohner, Janet Vorwald. *Livestock Guardians: Using Dogs, Donkeys, and Llamas to Protect Your Herd*. Storey's Working Animal series. North Adams, MA: Storey Publishing, 2007.

Rigg, Robin. "Livestock Guarding Dogs: Their Current Use World Wide." Occasional Paper 1, Species Survival Commission, International Union for the Conservation of Nature and Natural Resources, Gland, Switzerland, 2001.

Urbigkit, Cat. *Brave Dogs, Gentle Dogs: How They Guard Sheep*. Honesdale, PA: Boyds Mills Press, 2005.

To Fynn

For information about permission to reproduce selections
from this book, please contact permissions@highlights.com.

Boyds Mills Press, Inc.
An Imprint of Highlights
815 Church Street
Honesdale, Pennsylvania
Printed in China

ISBN: 978-1-59078-770-0

Library of Congress Control Number: 2011920697

First edition
The text of this book is set in ITC Clearface.

10 9 8 7 6 5 4 3 2